THE WAY OF THE CROSS

Plinio Corrêa de Oliveira

America Needs Fatima
P.O. Box 1868, York, PA, 17405

The America Needs Fatima Campaign is a special project of The American Society for the Defense of Tradition, Family and property to capture the heart and soul of America with the Fatima message. America Needs Fatima and The American Society for the Defense of Tradition, Family and Property are assumed names of The Foundation for a Christian Civilization, Inc.

Second edition
© 1998 by The America Needs Fatima Campaign
All rights reserved. Published 1990
Printed in the United States of America

Library of Congress Catalog Card Number: 90-81235
ISBN # 1-877905-16-X

O Sorrowful Mother,
in these times wherein the immense
majority of men flee from the sacrifice
inherent to perfect fulfillment
of all the commandments and counsels
of thy Divine Son,
obtain for all those who meditate
on this Way of the Cross
the necessary strength for each
to carry his cross
to the heights of Calvary.

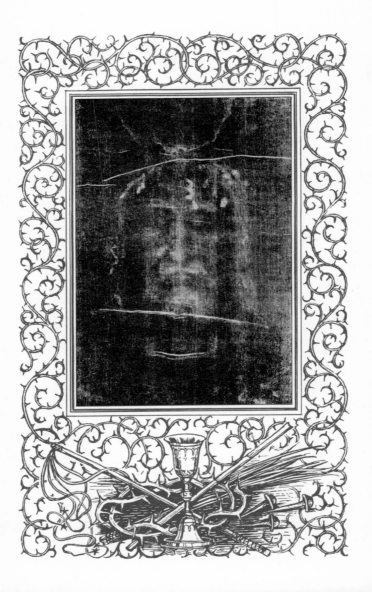

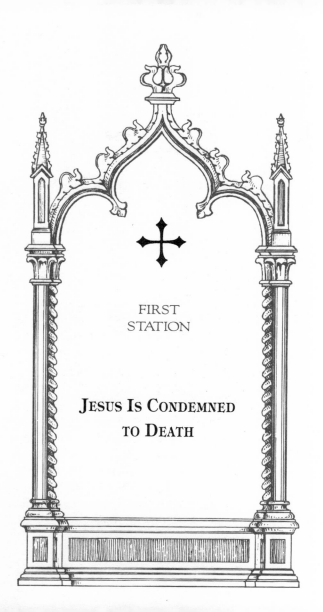

FIRST
STATION

**JESUS IS CONDEMNED
TO DEATH**

Jesus Is Condemned to Death

℣. We adore Thee, O Christ, and we bless Thee.

℟. Because by Thy holy Cross Thou hast redeemed the world.

THE judge who committed the most monstrous professional crime in all history was not impelled to do so by the excitement of any burning passion. Nor was he blinded by ideological hatred, by craving for new riches, or by the desire to please some great potentate. He was moved to condemn the Just One by fear—fear of losing his position for apparent lack of zeal for the prerogatives of Caesar; fear of causing himself political complications by having displeased the Jewish mob; and the instinctive fear of saying no, of doing the opposite of what has been asked of one, of facing the crowd with attitudes and opinions different from those that prevail there.

For a long time, O Lord, Thou didst fix him with that look which in one instant worked the salvation of Peter. It was a look through which one could see Thy supreme moral perfection, Thine infinite innocence. But he condemned Thee anyway.

O Lord, how many times have I imitated Pilate! How many times, out of ambition for personal advancement, have I permitted orthodoxy to be persecuted in my presence without saying a word. How many times have I stood by with my arms crossed at the fight and martyrdom of those who defend the Church! I did not have the courage to give them even a word of support because of an abominable slothfulness to face those who surrounded me, to say no to those around me, for fear of being "different from the others." As if Thou hadst created me, Lord, not to imitate Thee, but to slavishly imitate my companions.

In that painful moment of condemnation, Thou didst suffer for all cowards, for all weaklings, for all the lukewarm . . . for me, Lord.

My Jesus, pardon and mercy. By the fortitude Thou didst show me in braving unpopularity and facing the sentence of the Roman magistrate, cure the weakness of my soul.

Our Father. Hail Mary. Glory Be.

℣. Have mercy on us, Lord.

℟. Have mercy on us.

℣. May the souls of the faithful departed, through the mercy of God, rest in peace.

℟. Amen.

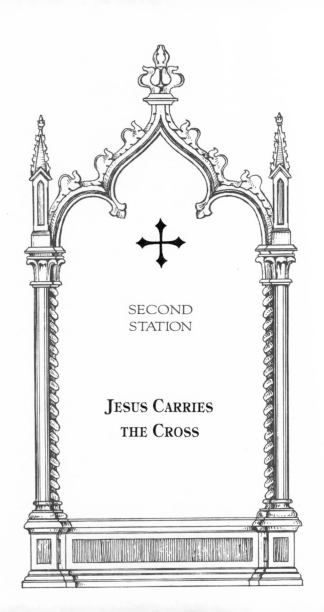

SECOND
STATION

JESUS CARRIES
THE CROSS

SECOND STATION

Jesus Carries the Cross

℣. We adore Thee, O Christ, and we bless Thee.

℟. Because by Thy holy Cross Thou hast redeemed the world.

THUS began, my adorable Lord, Thy walk to the place of immolation. It was not the wish of the Heavenly Father that Thou shouldst die by one fulminating blow. In Thy Passion, Thou hadst to teach us not only to die, but to face death. Facing it with serenity, with neither hesitation nor weakness, walking toward it, even with the resolute pace of a warrior advancing to combat—behold the admirable lesson Thou givest me.

In the face of pain, my God, how great is my cowardice. Sometimes I temporize before taking up my cross; sometimes I shrink back, neglecting an obligation. Finally I accept it, but so irksomely, so halfheartedly, that I seem to hate the burden that Thy will hast placed on my shoulders.

How often, on other occasions, do I close my eyes in order not to see the pain. I voluntarily blind myself with stupid optimism because I have not the courage to face the trial. And so I lie to myself: It is not true that the renunciation of a certain pleasure is an obligation for me in order not to fall into sin; it is not true that I must overcome a certain habit which favors my most deep-rooted passions; it is not true that I must abandon a certain group, a friendship which undermines and ruins my whole spiritual life. No, none of this is not true at all . . . I close my eyes, and I cast aside my cross.

My Jesus, pardon me so much sloth. By the wound which the Cross opened in Thy shoulder, cure, O Father of Mercies, the horrible wound I have opened in my soul through entire years lived in interior dissipation and self-indulgence!

Our Father. Hail Mary. Glory Be.

℣. Have mercy on us, Lord.

℞. Have mercy on us.

℣. May the souls of the faithful departed, through the mercy of God, rest in peace.

℞. Amen.

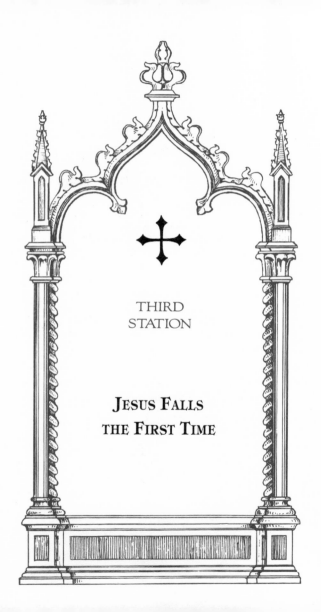

THIRD
STATION

**Jesus Falls
the First Time**

THIRD STATION

Jesus Falls the First Time

℣. We adore Thee, O Christ, and we bless Thee.

℞. Because by Thy holy Cross Thou hast redeemed the world.

WHAT then, Lord? Was it not justifiable for Thee to abandon Thy cross? By carrying it until all Thy strength was exhausted, until the insupportable weight of the wood hurled Thee to the ground, hadst Thou not clearly proved that it was impossible for Thee to continue? Thine obligation was fulfilled. Let the angels of heaven carry Thy cross for Thee now. Thou hast suffered in full measure all that was possible. What more wouldst Thou have to give?

Nevertheless, by acting in another way, Thou didst give my cowardice a sublime lesson. With Thy strength exhausted, Thou didst not renounce the burden but askest for yet more strength to carry the Cross once again. And Thou didst obtain it.

The life of a Christian is difficult today. To be obligated to struggle unremittingly against oneself in order to keep the Commandments seems to be an extravagant exception in a world that flaunts the joy of life in licentiousness and opulence. Heavy on our shoulders weighs the cross of fidelity to Thy Law, O Lord. At times, we seem to be out of breath.

In these moments of trial, we rationalize. We have already done all that we can. After all, a man's strength is so limited! God will take this into account. Come, let us drop the cross here by the roadside and sink cozily into a life of pleasure. Ah, many are the crosses abandoned alongside our ways, perhaps along my tracks!

Grant me, Jesus, the grace to continue to embrace my cross, even when I collapse under its weight. Grant me the grace to rise up again whenever I grow faint. Grant me, Lord, the supreme grace of never departing from the way by which I must reach the height of my own calvary.

Our Father. Hail Mary. Glory Be.

℣. Have mercy on us, Lord.

℟. Have mercy on us.

℣. May the souls of the faithful departed, through the mercy of God, rest in peace.

℟. Amen.

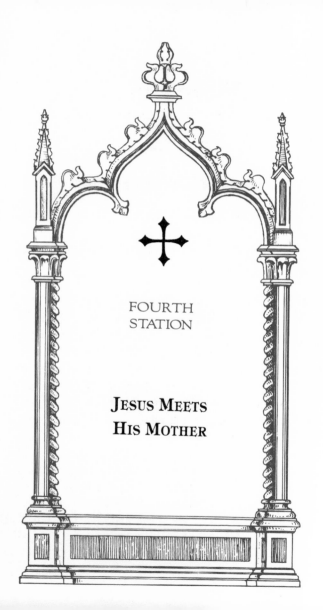

FOURTH
STATION

**JESUS MEETS
HIS MOTHER**

Jesus Meets His Mother

℣. We adore Thee, O Christ, and we bless Thee.

℟. Because by Thy holy Cross Thou hast redeemed the world.

WHO, my Lady, seeing thee shed such tears would dare to ask thee why thou weepest? Neither the earth, nor the sea, nor all the heavens can serve as a term of comparison to thy sorrow. Grant me, my Mother, at least a little of that sorrow. Grant me the grace to weep for Jesus with tears of sincere and profound compunction. Thou didst suffer in union with Jesus. Grant me the grace to suffer as He and thou didst suffer.

Thy greatest sorrow arose not from contemplating the inexpressible bodily sufferings of thy Divine Son. What are bodily evils in comparison with those of the spirit? If Jesus had suffered all of those torments while having at His side compassionate hearts! If His Sacred Heart had not been wounded enormously more by the most senseless, unjust, and blatant hatred than by the weight of the Cross and the brutalities that wounded His Body! Rather, He was assailed by the tumultuous manifestations of hatred and ingratitude of those whom He had loved: Two steps away was a leper whom He had healed; a little farther, a blind man to whom He had restored sight; farther along, a tormented soul to whom He had restored peace. All of them called for His death; all of them hated Him; all of them insulted Him. These caused Jesus immensely more suffering than did the inexpressible pains that weighed upon His Body.

Yet, there was worse. There was the worst of evils. There was sin: avowed sin, obtrusive sin, atrocious sin. If all those acts of ingratitude had been committed against the best of men but by some absurdity had not offended God . . . but they were committed against the God-man, and thus they constituted a supreme sin against all three Persons of the Blessed Trinity. This was the greatest evil of the injustice and the ingratitude.

This evil lies not so much in the offense against the rights of a benefactor but in the offense against God. Amidst so many and such great causes of sorrow, what caused Thee the most suffering, my Divine Redeemer, and thee, Blessed Mother, was certainly sin.

And I? Am I mindful of my sins? Do I remember, for example, my first sin, or my most recent sin? What of the hour when I committed it, of the place, of the persons who surrounded me, the motives which led me to sin? If I had thought of the magnitude of the offense which a sin causes Thee, would I have dared to disobey Thee, my Lord?

O my Mother, by the sorrow of that holy meeting, obtain for me the grace to have always before my eyes Jesus suffering and wounded, exactly as thou seest Him in this step of the Passion.

Our Father. Hail Mary. Glory Be.

℣. Have mercy on us, Lord.

℟. Have mercy on us.

℣. May the souls of the faithful departed, through the mercy of God, rest in peace.

℟. Amen.

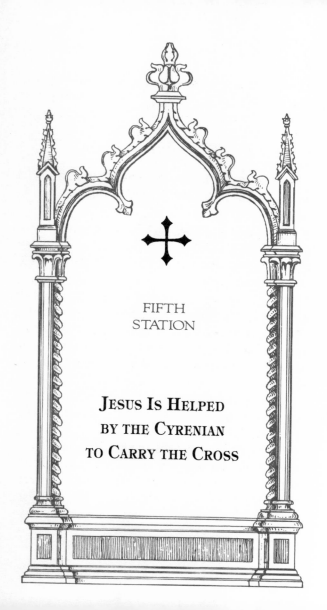

FIFTH
STATION

**Jesus Is Helped
by the Cyrenian
to Carry the Cross**

FIFTH STATION

Jesus Is Helped by the Cyrenian to Carry the Cross

℣. We adore Thee, O Christ, and we bless Thee.

℟. Because by Thy holy Cross Thou hast redeemed the world.

WHO was Simon? What is known of him, except that he was of Cyrene? And what do most men know of Cyrene other than it was the land of Simon? Both the city and the man emerged from obscurity and entered into glory, the most exalted glory, sacred glory, at a moment when the thoughts of the Cyrenian were far from all this.

He was walking carelessly along the road. He was thinking only about those petty problems and petty interests that make up the trivial lives of the majority of men. But Thou, Lord, didst cross his path with Thy wounds, Thy Cross, Thy immense sorrow. Simon had to take a position in regard to Thee. The soldiers forced him to carry the Cross with Thee. He could carry it with bad humor, indifferent to Thee, trying to please the people by means of some new way of increasing the torments Thou didst suffer in soul and body; or he could carry it with love, with compassion, scorning the mob, trying to relieve Thy suffering, taking some of it on himself so that Thou wouldst suffer a little less. The Cyrenian preferred to suffer with Thee. For this reason his name has been repeated with love, with gratitude, with holy envy, for two thousand years, by all men of faith, all over the face of the earth, and so it will continue until the end of time.

Thou hast passed also along my path, my Jesus. Thou didst pass when Thou called me out of the darkness of paganism and into the bosom of Thy Church through Holy Baptism. Thou didst pass also when my parents taught me to pray. Thou didst pass again when in the Catechism class I began to open my soul to the true doctrine, Catholic and orthodox. Thou didst pass in my first Confession, in my First Communion, in all of the moments when I vacillated and Thou didst help me, in all of the moments when I fell and Thou didst pick me up, in all of the moments when I asked and Thou didst hear me.

And I, Lord? Even now Thou passest by me in this exercise of the Way of the Cross. And what do I do when Thou passest by me?

Our Father. Hail Mary. Glory Be.

℣. Have mercy on us, Lord.

℟. Have mercy on us.

℣. May the souls of the faithful departed, through the mercy of God, rest in peace.

℟. Amen.

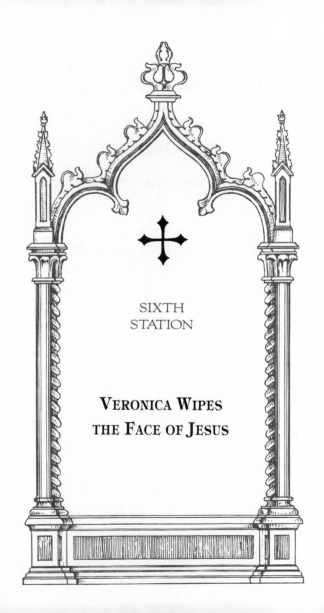

SIXTH
STATION

**VERONICA WIPES
THE FACE OF JESUS**

Veronica Wipes the Face of Jesus

℣. We adore Thee, O Christ, and we bless Thee.

℟. Because by Thy holy Cross Thou hast redeemed the world.

ONE would say at first glance that never was there a greater reward in all of history. Indeed, what king ever held in his hands a cloth more precious than that veil? What general, a more august banner? What gesture of courage and dedication was recompensed with a more extraordinary favor?

But there is a grace which is more valuable than having the Holy Face of the Savior stamped on a veil. The representation of the Divine Face was made on the veil as in a painting. In the Holy Roman Catholic and Apostolic Church, His Face is reflected as in a mirror.

In her institutions, in her doctrine, in her laws,

in her unity, in her universality, in her unsurpassable catholicity, the Church is a true mirror in which our Divine Savior is reflected.

And we, all of us, have the grace of belonging to the Church, of being living stones of the Church!

How we ought to give thanks for this favor! Let us not forget, however, that noblesse oblige. Belonging to the Church is a very great and very demanding thing. We must think as the Church thinks, have the Mind of the Church, proceed as the Church wishes in all the circumstances of our lives. This supposes a real Catholic sense, an authentic and complete purity of customs, and a profound and sincere piety. In other words it supposes the sacrifice of an entire lifetime.

And what is the reward? *"Christianus alter Christus."* I will be in an eminent way a reproduction of Christ Himself. The likeness of Christ, vivid and sacred, will be imprinted, on my own soul.

Ah, Lord, if the grace granted to Veronica is great, how much greater is the favor that Thou dost promise me!

I ask of Thee strength and resoluteness so that I may obtain this favor by being faithful in every trial.

Our Father. Hail Mary. Glory Be.

℣. Have mercy on us, Lord.

℟. Have mercy on us.

℣. May the souls of the faithful departed, through the mercy of God, rest in peace.

℟. Amen.

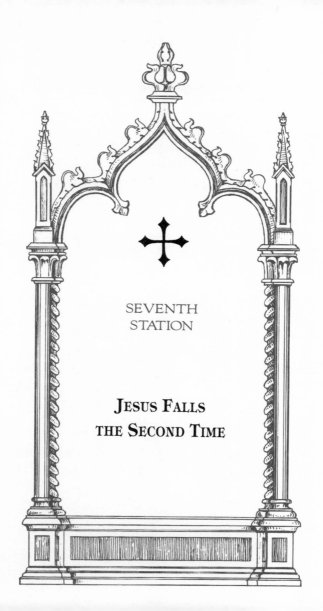

SEVENTH
STATION

**JESUS FALLS
THE SECOND TIME**

Jesus Falls the Second Time

℣. We adore Thee, O Christ, and we bless Thee.

℟. Because by Thy holy Cross Thou hast redeemed the world.

TO fall, to be stretched out flat on the ground, to be at the feet of all in order to publicly manifest that now Thou hast no more strength; to these humiliations Thou didst choose to subject Thyself, Lord, as a lesson for me. No one felt sorrow for Thee. Rather, they redoubled their insults and abuses. All the while, Thy grace sought in vain in the interior of those hardened hearts for a movement of pity.

Even at that moment, Thou didst desire to continue Thy Passion for the salvation of men. What men? All men, including those who were doing everything possible to increase Thy suffering.

And so, Lord, I must continue my apostolate, even when all my works have tumbled to the ground, even when all have joined together to attack me, even when the ingratitude and perversity of those to whom I have wished to do good have turned against me.

I will not be so weak as to change my path to please them. My ways can be only Thy ways, the ways of orthodoxy, of purity, of austerity. Following Thy ways I shall suffer for them. With my imperfect sorrows united to Thy perfect sorrow, Thine infinitely precious sorrow, I shall continue to do good for them so that they may save themselves, or so that the rejected graces may accumulate over them like burning coals clamoring for punishment. Thus Thou didst with the nation which committed the deicide and so also wilt Thou do with those who will reject Thee until the end of time.

Our Father. Hail Mary. Glory Be.

℣. Have mercy on us, Lord.

℟. Have mercy on us.

℣. May the souls of the faithful departed, through the mercy of God, rest in peace.

℟. Amen.

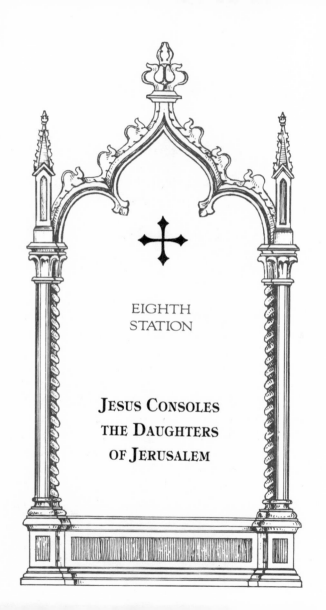

EIGHTH
STATION

**JESUS CONSOLES
THE DAUGHTERS
OF JERUSALEM**

Jesus Consoles the Daughters of Jerusalem

℣. We adore Thee, O Christ, and we bless Thee.

℟. Because by Thy holy Cross Thou hast redeemed the world.

T HERE were at that time good souls, who, realizing the enormity of the sin being committed, feared the divine justice.

Am I not witness to a certain sin like that? Is it not true that today Our Lord Jesus Christ and His Holy Church are disobeyed, abandoned, betrayed? Is it not true that the laws, institutions, morals, and ways of the people are more and more hostile to Jesus Christ? Is it not true that Our Lady spoke at Fatima, pointing out all of these sins and asking for penance?

But where is that penance? How many are there who really see these sins and who try to point them out, denounce them, fight them, dispute every inch of their advance, raise up against them a whole crusade of ideas, of acts, of force if it be necessary? And how many are there who are capable of unfurling the standard of absolute and flawless orthodoxy in the very places where impiety or false piety struts? How many are they who live in union with the Church during this moment that is tragic as the Passion was tragic, this crucial moment of history when all mankind is choosing to be for Christ or against Christ?

Oh, my God, how many myopic ones there are who prefer neither to see nor to foresee the reality which lies plainly before their eyes! How much false peacefulness, how much trifling well-being, how many petty routine pleasures! How many tasty dishes of pottage to be eaten!

Grant us, Jesus, the grace not to be of that number. Grant us the grace to follow Thy counsel, that is, to weep for ourselves and for our own. Give us not just a few sterile tears, but grant us a flood of tears, which, poured out at Thy feet and made fertile by Thee, may become for us forgiveness, strength for the apostolate, for the fight, and for acts of intrepidity.

Our Father. Hail Mary. Glory Be.

℣. Have mercy on us, Lord.

℟. Have mercy on us.

℣. May the souls of the faithful departed, through the mercy of God, rest in peace.

℟. Amen.

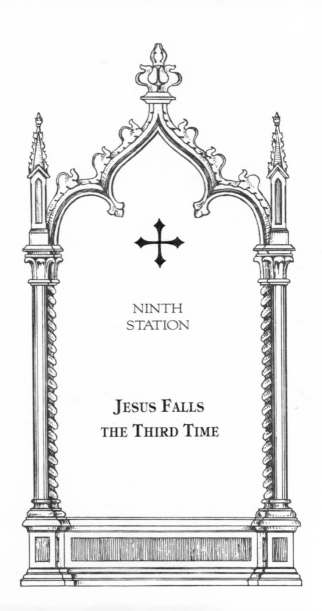

NINTH
STATION

**JESUS FALLS
THE THIRD TIME**

Ninth Station

Jesus Falls the Third Time

℣. We adore Thee, O Christ, and we bless Thee.

℟. Because by Thy holy Cross Thou hast redeemed the world.

THOU art now, my Lord, more tired, more drained, more wounded, more bloodless than ever. What awaits Thee? Hast Thou reached the end? No. Precisely the worst is yet to come. The most atrocious crime is still to be perpetrated. The worst sorrows still must be suffered. Thou art on the ground a third time but, nonetheless, all that is behind Thee is no more than a preface. And, behold, Thou once again movest that Body which is but one wound. The seemingly impossible is being achieved, once more Thou slowly riseth to Thy feet, even though every movement increases Thy pain. There Thou art, Lord, standing once again . . .

with Thy Cross. Thou didst know how to find new strength, new energy, and Thou didst continue. Three falls, three equal lessons in perseverance, each more poignant and more expressive than the last.

Why so much insistence? Because our cowardice is insistent. We resolve to take up our crosses, but cowardice always comes charging back. So that cowardice might find no pretext in our weakness, Thou didst desire to repeat the lesson three times Thyself.

Yes, it is true: Our weakness cannot serve us as a pretext. Grace, which God never refuses, can do that which mere natural strength would never be able to do.

God wishes to be served to the last breath, to the exhaustion of the last drop of strength, and He multiplies our capacities for suffering and doing so that our dedication may reach the extreme limit of the unforeseeable, the improbable, the miraculous. The measure of the love of God is to love Him without measure, said Saint Francis de Sales. The measure of fighting for God consists in fighting without measure, it may be said.

But, I, how quickly I tire! In my works of apostolate the least sacrifice holds me back, the least effort terrifies me, the slightest combat puts me to flight. I like the apostolate, it is true. The apostolate I like is one entirely in accordance with my likings and fancies, to which I give myself when I wish, as I wish, and because I wish. After that I consider I have done a great almsdeed for God.

But God is not satisfied with this. For the Church He wants my whole life, He wants organization, He wants sagacity, He wants intrepidity, He wants the innocence of the dove and the cunning of the serpent, the sweetness of the sheep and the irresistible and overwhelming wrath of the lion. If it be necessary to sacrifice my career, friendships, family ties, petty vanities, and inveterate habits, to serve Our Lord, I must do so. For this step of the Passion teaches me that we must give everything to God, absolutely everything, and after having given everything we ought to give our very lives as well.

Our Father. Hail Mary. Glory Be.

℣. Have mercy on us, Lord.

℟. Have mercy on us.

℣. May the souls of the faithful departed, through the mercy of God, rest in peace.

℟. Amen.

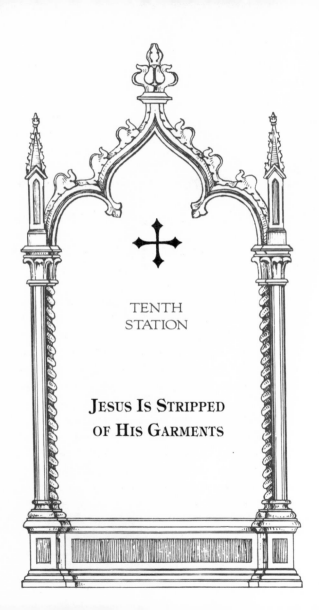

TENTH
STATION

**JESUS IS STRIPPED
OF HIS GARMENTS**

Jesus Is Stripped of His Garments

℣. We adore Thee, O Christ, and we bless Thee.

℟. Because by Thy holy Cross Thou has redeemed the world.

EVERYTHING, yes, absolutely everything. We must suffer even shame for the love of God and for the salvation of souls.

The proof of this: He who is Purity par excellence was stripped, and the impure mocked Him in His purity. Our Lord endured these jests of impurity.

Does it not appear insignificant for Him—having already endured so many torments—to endure these jests as well? But this lesson, like the others, was necessary for us. Because of the scorn of a maidservant, Saint Peter denied Our Lord. How many men have forsaken Our Lord for fear of ridicule! If men go to war and face gunfire and death to avoid being mocked as cowards, is it not perfectly true that certain men fear laughter more than anything?

The Divine Master faced ridicule. He taught us that nothing is ridiculous when it is in the line of virtue and goodness.

Teach me, Lord, to reflect in myself the majesty of Thy countenance and the strength of Thy perseverance when the wicked wish to use the arm of ridicule against me.

Our Father. Hail Mary. Glory Be.

℣. Have mercy on us, Lord.

℟. Have mercy on us.

℣. May the souls of the faithful departed, through the mercy of God, rest in peace.

℟. Amen.

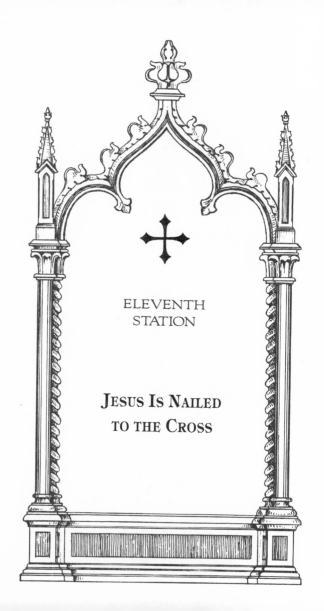

ELEVENTH
STATION

**Jesus Is Nailed
to the Cross**

ELEVENTH STATION

Jesus Is Nailed to the Cross

℣. We adore Thee, O Christ, and we bless
Thee.

℟. Because by Thy holy Cross Thou hast
redeemed the world.

FOR Thee, my Lord, impiety chose the worst
of final torments. The worst, yes, because
it is that which causes one to die slowly, that
which produces the greatest sufferings, and that
which, being reserved for the most abject crimi-
nals, was the most infamous. Everything was
prepared by hell to make Thee suffer in body
and soul. Does this immense hatred not have
some lesson for me? Woe betide me—who never
will understand it sufficiently—if I do not become holy.

Between Thee and the devil, between good and
evil, between truth and error, there is a profound, irreconcilable, eternal hatred. Darkness

hates the light, the children of darkness hate the children of light; the fight between the two sides will endure until the consummation of the ages, and there will never be peace between the race of the Woman and the race of the Serpent.

In order to understand the immeasurable extension and immensity of this hatred, it is necessary to contemplate all that it dared to do. There is the Son of God, transformed, in the words of Scripture, into a leper in whom nothing is sound; a being who writhes like a worm under the effect of the pain; detested, abandoned, nailed to a cross between two common thieves. The Son of God: what grandeur—infinite, unimaginable, absolute—is contained in those words! Behold, in spite of all, what hatred has dared to do against the Son of God!

The whole history of the world, the whole history of the Church is nothing but this inexorable struggle between those who are of God and those who are of the devil, between those who are of the Virgin and those who are of the Serpent. It is a struggle in which there are not merely mistakes of the intellect nor only weakness in the angelic and human hosts which follow Satan, but also malice—deliberate, culpable, sinful malice.

Behold that which needs to be said, commented on, remembered, emphasized, proclaimed, and once more remembered at the foot of the Cross. For we are such, and liberalism has disfigured us to such a point that we are always inclined to forget this truth absolutely inseparable from the contemplation of the Passion.

Well did the Virgin of virgins, the Mother of Sorrows, know this, she who participated in the Passion along with her Son. Well did the virgin apostle know this, he who at the foot of the Cross received Mary as his Mother, thus receiving the greatest legacy ever given a man to receive, because there are certain truths which God has reserved for the pure and which He denies to the impure.

My Mother, in the moment in which even the good thief merited forgiveness, I ask that Jesus forgive me for all the blindness with which I have considered all the works of darkness being plotted around me.

Our Father. Hail Mary. Glory Be.

℣. Have mercy on us, Lord.

℟. Have mercy on us.

℣. May the souls of the faithful departed, through the mercy of God, rest in peace.

℟. Amen.

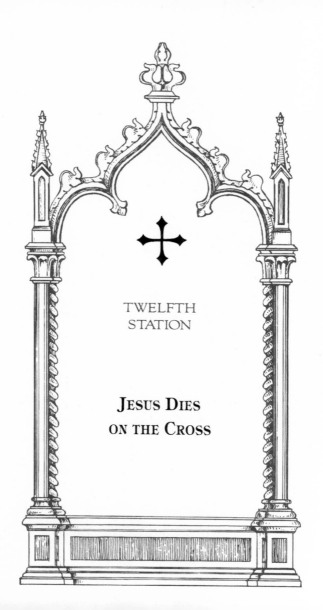

TWELFTH
STATION

**JESUS DIES
ON THE CROSS**

TWELFTH STATION

Jesus Dies on the Cross

℣. We adore Thee, O Christ, and we bless Thee.

℞. Because by Thy holy Cross Thou hast redeemed the world.

F INALLY the apex of all pains is reached. It is a summit so high that it is lost in the clouds of mystery. The physical pains having reached their limits, the moral sufferings having attained their zenith, a mysterious torment must be the climax of such an inexpressible pain: "My God, my God, why hast Thou forsaken me?" In a certain mysterious way, the Word Incarnate Himself was afflicted by that spiritual torture of abandonment in which the soul receives no consolations from God. Such was this torment that He of Whom the Evangelists record not a single word of pain uttered that piercing cry: "My God, my God, why hast Thou forsaken me?"

Yes, why? Why did this happen if He was Innocence itself? This terrible abandonment was followed by death and the perturbation of all of nature. The sun was darkened. The sky lost its splendor. The earth quaked. The veil of the temple was rent in two. Desolation covered the whole universe.

Why? To redeem man. To destroy sin. To open the gates of heaven. The height of suffering was the height of victory. Death was put to death. The purified earth was like a great field which had been cleared so that the Church might be built on it.

All of this, then, was to save, to save men, to save this man who I am. My salvation was purchased at such a price. I will spare myself no sacrifice to secure that salvation so precious. By the water and the Blood that came forth from Thy divine Side, by the wound of Thy Heart, by the sorrows of Mary Most Holy, grant me, O Jesus, the strength to detach myself from the persons and things that can separate me from Thee. Today they die, nailed to the Cross, all the friendships, all the affections, all the ambitions, all the delights that have separated me from Thee.

Our Father. Hail Mary. Glory Be.

℣. Have mercy on us, Lord.

℟. Have mercy on us.

℣. May the souls of the faithful departed, through the mercy of God, rest in peace.

℟. Amen.

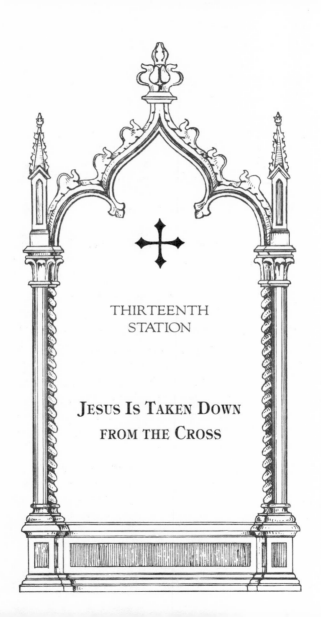

THIRTEENTH
STATION

**JESUS IS TAKEN DOWN
FROM THE CROSS**

Thirteenth Station

Jesus Is Taken Down from the Cross

℣. We adore Thee, O Christ, and we bless Thee.

℟. Because by Thy holy Cross Thou hast redeemed the world.

THE repose of the sepulcher awaits Thee, Lord. In the shadows of death, Thou dost open heaven to the just in limbo, while on earth around Thy Mother, a few faithful ones gather to give Thee funeral honors. In the silence of those moments, there is the first glimmer of an aborning hope. Those first acts of homage being offered to Thee mark the inauguration of a series of acts of love by redeemed mankind that will continue until the end of time.

It is a scene of sorrow and desolation, yet of great peace as well. It is a scene wherein something of the triumph is presaged in the ineffable cares with which Thy Divine Body is treated.

Yes, those pious souls condole with one another, but there is something about them that makes one foresee in Thee the glorious Victor.

May I also, Lord, in the great desolations of the Church, be always faithful; may I be present in the saddest hours, unshakably preserving the certainty that Thy Spouse will triumph by the fidelity of the good because Thy protection assists her.

Our Father. Hail Mary. Glory Be.

℣. Have mercy on us, Lord.

℟. Have mercy on us.

℣. May the souls of the faithful departed, through the mercy of God, rest in peace.

℟. Amen.

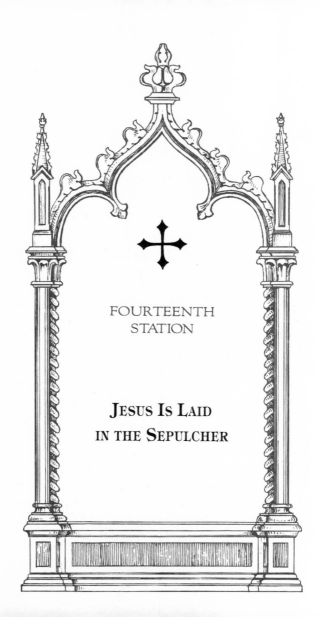

FOURTEENTH
STATION

Jesus Is Laid
in the Sepulcher

FOURTEENTH STATION

Jesus Is Laid in the Sepulcher

℣. We adore Thee, O Christ, and we bless Thee.

℟. Because by Thy holy Cross Thou hast redeemed the world.

THE stone is rolled into place. Everything seems to have ended. But, it is the moment when everything begins. It is the regrouping of the Apostles. It is the rebirth of dedication, of hope. Easter draws near.

At the same time, the hatred of Thine enemies surrounds the sepulcher, Mary Most Holy, and the Apostles.

But they do not fear. In a little while the dawn of the Resurrection will break.

Let me not fear either, Lord Jesus, not fear when everything seems irremediably lost, not fear when all the power on earth appears to be in the hands of Thine enemies. Let me not fear because I am at the feet of Our Lady where the true followers of Thy Church always regroup, and will always regroup, for new victories.

Our Father. Hail Mary. Glory Be.

℣. Have mercy on us, Lord.

℟. Have mercy on us.

℣. May the souls of the faithful departed, through the mercy of God, rest in peace.

℟. Amen.

*"Finally, my
Immaculate Heart will triumph."*

ABOUT THE AUTHOR

PLINIO CORRÊA DE OLIVEIRA, born in São Paulo, Brazil in 1908, received his doctorate from the Law School of the University of São Paulo. On leaving the university, he began his professional and public career, at the same time becoming prominent as the most outstanding leader of the Catholic movement of São Paulo.

At 24 he was elected to the Constitutional Assembly, becoming its youngest member and the one receiving the greatest number of votes.

Shortly thereafter, he assumed the chair of History of Civilization at the University College, a branch of the University of São Paulo, and later became professor of Modern and Contemporary History in the Colleges of São Bento and Sedes Sapientiae, which would become part of the Pontifical Catholic University of São Paulo.

He was director of the Catholic weekly *Legionário*, and has held an outstanding place on the editorial staff of the cultural monthly *Catolicismo* since its founding in 1951. A columnist for the large daily *Folha de S. Paulo*, his articles are also published in several other organs of the Brazilian press and of other countries in the Americas.

In 1960 he founded the Brazilian TFP, and has been president of its National Council ever since.

The American TFP and the other autonomous kindred TFPs and TFP Bureaus now in twenty-two countries on five continents were inspired by the book

Revolution and Counter-Revolution and other works of Professor Corrêa de Oliveira.

They are comprised of militant Catholics shocked at the advance of the Catholic left. The TFP works to alert the American public and our leaders about the increasing and noxious influence of socialist and communist principles in intellectual life. The TFP, however, is not a negative movement that is simply anticommunist, antisocialist, and the like. From its very founding, the TFP has presented its fight in a positive manner, dedicating itself to promoting tradition, family and property, three values especially targeted by the destructive action of the left and that the TFP believes should be particularly emphasized and understood by the general public. Sound American traditions and the institutions of the family and private property are pillars of Christian civilization in our country.

According to Canon Law, the TFP can be classified as an assocation of Catholic inspiration, comprised of laymen acting in the temporal sphere under their own responsibility (Code of Canon Law, canon 227). Nevertheless, the TFP has the traditional teaching of the Supreme Magisterium of the Church as its guiding light.

It carries out a continual program of educational activities for the general public and particularly for the youth. For this purpose, it promotes (1) lecture tours, (2) seminars and conferences, (3) doctrinal and historical books, (4) studies that expound its ideals and refute the theses of its adversaries, and (5) audiovisual presentations. For more information, please write or call: The American TFP, P.O. Box 1868, York, PA, 17405. Tel.: 717-225-7147 Fax: 717-225-7382